ACKNOWLEDGMENTS

Without the University Library at the University of Illinois at Urbana-Champaign, I don't know how I would have obtained all the resources that I used to research this book. The books (especially those in French), Josephine's films from the twenties and thirties, and the musical and spoken recordings (some of which I listened to on obscure and obsolete technological devices also provided by the library) were invaluable. I was also so fortunate to have visited the Sheldon Art Galleries in Saint Louis, Missouri, in 2006, which presented the exhibit *Josephine Baker: Image and Icon*, curated by Olivia Lahs-Gonzales.

DEDICATION

In memory of my magnificent mother Dolores M. Hruby —P. H. P.

For Josephine —C. R.

SPECIAL THANKS

To Lovisa Brown, Director of Education at the Museum of the African Diaspora, for her department's generous consultation in the making of this book.

Library of Congress Cataloging-in-Publication Data
Powell, Patricia Hruby, 1951-
Josephine : the dazzling life of Josephine Baker /
By Patricia Hruby Powell ; Illustrated by Christian
Robinson.
pages cm
ISBN 978-1-4521-0314-3 (alk. paper)
1. Baker, Josephine, 1906-1975—Juvenile literature.
2. Dancers—France—Biography—Juvenile literature.
3. African American entertainers—France—Biography—
Juvenile literature. I. Robinson, Christian, illustrator.
II. Title.
GV1785.B3P68 2014
792.802'8092—dc23
[B]
2012030440

Manufactured in Canada.

Design by Jennifer Tolo Pierce.
Typeset in Neutra Text, Neutra Display, and Monterey BT.
The illustrations in this book were rendered in acrylic
on paper.

10 9 8 7 6 5 4 3 2

Chronicle Books LLC
680 Second Street, San Francisco, California 94107

Chronicle Books—we see things differently. Become part
of our community at www.chroniclekids.com.

JOSEPHINE

The Dazzling Life of Josephine Baker

WORDS BY
PATRICIA HRUBY POWELL

PICTURES BY
CHRISTIAN ROBINSON

chronicle books · san francisco

"I shall dance all my life. . . .
I would like to die, breathless,
spent, at the end of a dance."

—JOSEPHINE BAKER, 1927

JOSEPHINE

      danced a sizzling flapper dance—
the Charleston.

      Knees SQUEEZE, now FLY
        heels flap and chop
            arms scissor and splay
      eyes swivel and pop.

      Josephine, all
            RAZZMATAZZ,
erupted into the Roaring Twenties—
        a VOLCANO.

America wasn't ready for Josephine,
      the colored superstar.

      PARIS WAS.

THE BEGINNING

1906–1917

Josephine—
born poor,
out of wedlock
in honky-tonk town—
      rambunctious
SAINT LOUIS, Missouri—
home of barrelhouses,
nickel shots of whisky,
and gambling halls—
home of
      RAGTIME MUSIC—
raggedy black music—
gotta-make-the-rent music—
lift-my-soul music—
GOLDEN-AGE music.

Josephine's mama scrubbed floors,
but would've rather been
      DANCING—
where you were free of
how-to-pay-the-rent,
where you could be right there
in your body
nowhere else, where you could
let your body LAUGH.
Or CRY.

She dreamt of dancing
alongside acrobats, magicians, animals,
honky-tonk bands, you name it.
Called it VAUDEVILLE,
the most popular entertainment of the day.

Josephine sat on Mama's knee and sponged up that funky music
through her ears, her body.
Her SOUL.

Mama called her TUMPY, that round baby girl, after Humpty Dumpty.
With her first breath, she made faces.
As soon as she walked, she DANCED.
When she talked, she told stories
and kept on all her life—

     to get attention,

          to entertain,

               to suit her mood.

She told THIS STORY:
Walking home from church one day,
she stepped on a rusty nail.
Her small leg swelled.
Doctor said, AMPUTATE!
Josephine screamed to keep her leg.
How was she going to dance with only one leg?
She screamed till she fainted.

When she woke she felt for her leg.
Yes, yes.
    There it was.
            She could have DANCED FOR JOY.

    Tumpy and family moved through
            the slums of Saint Louie,
like a band of VAGABONDS,
            from shack to shack.

They all six slept in one bed—
        Daddy and Mama, heads one way,
four kids, the other way—
        newspapers covering the window.

Tumpy was
        MAMA, DADDY, and SANTA
    to the little ones.
Old ropes for jumping, bits of chalk for hopscotch,
            and cast-off dolls,
she wrapped in discarded paper—
        Christmas presents for Richard, Margaret,
            and Willie Mae.

    Mama washed laundry. For other people.
Tumpy scrubbed alongside Mama.

And Tumpy DANCED.

*"I didn't have any stockings. . . .
I danced to keep warm."*

She flung her arms,
            she flung her legs.
Like she flung her heart and her soul.
'Cause DANCIN' makes you HAPPY
            when nothin' else will.

LEAVIN' WITH THE SHOW

1917–1921

RACE RIOTS—white against Negro—
ERUPTED across the river,
   across from her shantytown.
'Cause some Negroes earned better wages than whites.
At better jobs.

WHITE RABBLE-ROUSERS spread lies—
said Negroes were invading white neighborhoods
to steal, rape, and murder.
White folks got scared.
Those ugly rumors incited some white folks
to beat, murder, and burn BLACK EAST SAINT LOUIS.

JOSEPHINE saw colored people
        —beaten—
fleeing their homes
        across the bridge over the Mississippi River
to Saint Louis.
                To her neighborhood.

            Fear grasped hold of her heart
and squeezed tight
            the core of a volcano.
            Anger heated and boiled into steam,
pressing HOT
                in a place DEEP IN HER SOUL.

Later she'd let the steam out
in little poofs.

POOF!

A funny face.
That used to be fear.

POOF!

She'd mock a gesture.
That used to be anger.
She'd turn it into dance.

AH, VERY WITTY.

Josephine delivered laundry for Grandma.
And for Mama.
She cleaned and babysat.

She earned pennies.
           PENNIES added up to NICKELS.
Put three nickels together
and Tumpy went to the
           BOOKER T. WASHINGTON THEATER—
       the Negro theater—

the place where Ma Rainey sang and Bessie Smith wailed,
the place where dancers hoofed, loose-limbed,
and comedians made you laugh.

In those days, Negroes entertained Negroes one place.
Whites entertained whites another place.
That's how it was.
           SEGREGATED.

TUMPY got the kids on her street
to dance and sing on a stage of crates—
a makeshift stage—
their very own VAUDEVILLE.
Tumpy starred, of course.
She danced the "ITCH"
            and the "MESS AROUND."

JOSEPHINE JOINED THE JONES FAMILY,
a ragtag trio DANCING and PLAYING in the streets,
earning spare change.

Papa Jones played the big horn,
Mama Jones, the trumpet,
daughter Doll played fiddle.
Josephine played SLIDE TROMBONE.
She danced.
She sang.

She SHOUTED and HOLLERED out on the street.

A vivacious vaudeville troupe,
THE DIXIE STEPPERS,
booked at the Booker T. Washington Theater,
needed an extra act.
The Jones family, performing outside,
won the job.

Off the street and onto the stage,
Josephine danced like she was
ON FIRE.
She arched her back and flipped her tail like a rooster,
she flapped and pumped,
dancing the "turkey trot"
SO FINE
that the Dixie Steppers asked her
to step along with them.

So long, Jones family.
Josephine was steppin' out.

YESSIR, she soared over the stage as Cupid,
god of love, with leaping legs and little wings.

Hooked on wires,
she held bow and arrow.
But her wires got crossed.
Couldn't get down.
Hanging in midair,
she rolled her eyes like shooting marbles,
flailed those long legs.

WHAT A CLOWN!

"Seeing everybody
looking at me
electrified me."

The audience laughed themselves to tears.
They STOMPED.
They CLAPPED.
Just a kid, thirteen,
and Josephine loved that crazy applause.

The Dixie Steppers, ready to leave Saint Louis
to set off on tour,
thought Josephine was too young
to leave her home.

Josephine didn't.
She said to her kid sister Margaret,

"Cross your heart . . .
swear you won't tell Mama . . .
I'm leavin' with the show . . ."

And Josephine set out with the Dixie Steppers.
She'd CONQUER THE WORLD and show 'em all.
She'd be rich,
she'd be famous.
She'd even send money home.

The Dixie Steppers took the train
down the MISSISSIPPI
    down to NEW ORLEANS,
dancing, singing, and partying
    all the way
through the land of the Ku Klux Klan,
where hostile white faces hid under white hoods,

where while folk threatened colored folk,
where whites lived apart,
    segregated from colored,
where signs for one latrine read WHITE ladies
and for another, COLORED women,
where a white person wouldn't sell you
a cup of coffee.
Because you were
NEGRO.

They performed on the black vaudeville circuit,
in RAMSHACKLE theaters
and OPEN-AIR hollows,
but there was no place to hook up Cupid.

So, instead of dancing,
Josephine became the DRESSER.
She helped dress the dancers down in New Orleans.
Until her usefulness ran out.

And who just happened to be in town,
but the ragtag JONES FAMILY—
Papa, Mama, and Doll.

The Dixie Steppers said,

STAY HERE WITH THE JONESES, JOSEPHINE,

'cause you're not stage material.

But that didn't suit Josephine's plan

to conquer the world.

Before the Dixie Steppers' train steamed out of the station,

Josephine hid in a costume trunk,

A STOWAWAY KID.

She LURCHED and BOUNCED and BRUISED
    inside that trunk.
The train screeched to a stop
            twenty-five miles down the line.
    She whimpered
            and climbed out.

The Dixie Steppers scolded her,
            consoled her,
then took her back into the fold.

        She begged the director, Mr. Bob Russell,
could she PLEASE DANCE on stage.
            She knew every dance.
    Every song.

Mr. Russell said her skin was too light
            to fit in with the other girls.

*"To the whites I looked chocolate,
to the blacks, like a pinky."*

But Mr. Russell, tired of her begging,
let her join the chorus line.

HOORAH.

    Josephine danced on stage after stage,
sang to the crowds,
but was kept out of restaurants, hotels,
and train stations
    for WHITES ONLY.

Josephine's VOLCANIC CORE heated,
but the comic in her got funnier,
like a hot steam release.

POOF.

The chorus kicked forward,
        she kicked backward.

POP.

They strutted,
        Josephine shimmied instead.

The hoofers in the chorus SCOWLED
but the audience laughed.
Josephine stepped out of time
at the end of the chorus line,
        dancing with the Dixie Steppers
                all the way up to Philadelphia,
where the Dixie Steppers
    tired of the road,
                went their separate ways.

MY FACE ISN'T MADE FOR SLEEPING

1921–1925

JOSEPHINE, just a tall skinny kid, fifteen,
on her own
          in the city of Philadelphia,
      met Willie Baker, Pullman porter,
handsome in his gray uniform and red cap.
          And married him.

      Now she was
                Josephine Baker.

      She heard about
the first all-black show
          on Broadway—White Theater Street,
New York City, USA.

Shuffle Along,
          performed by Negro folk—
in those segregated times—
                somehow broke onto Broadway.
And the white folk
                loved it.
SOUNDED GOOD TO JOSEPHINE.

Bound for Broadway,
       she rode that train ALL ALONE,
       strangers packed in beside her,
wondering where'd she go once she got there,
             CRYING
       every one of those ninety miles from Philly—
where she'd left sweet safe Willie.

She got off the train in NEW YORK at night
       with nothing to eat, nowhere to sleep.
       She found a park bench,
tucked her bundle of clothes under her head,
           and slept.

She awoke
DAZZLED by the big city and filled with hope,

walked straight to the theater,
BOLD as a SHOUT and auditioned for
Mr. Sissle, the producer:
　　　"Sorry, too small, too thin, too dark."

"Wasn't there any place in the world
where color didn't matter?"

But JOSEPHINE got the job
dressing the dancers. AGAIN.
She learned every dance.
Every song, too.

Just in case.

"Brush, fasten, unfasten, button, unbutton.
The dancers looked discouragingly healthy."

But one night
a dancer didn't show up.
That's all it took.
Josephine STEPPED IN FRONT of
the audience.

"When I saw those watching faces a giddiness swept over me . . . I let the music carry me away. The audience whistled and clapped."

At the END of the CHORUS LINE,
she stumbled off balance on elastic legs—
on purpose—
looked up in surprise,
dropped her elbows
like limp washcloths,
CROSSED HER EYES,
flashed a smile.
And the audience LAUGHED.

Josephine jutted out her hip, flirted and grinned,
and STOLE THE SPOTLIGHT from Eva, the star.
The audience howled.
Eva, the chorus, the director—
all raged at Josephine.
But the reviews raved, "A BORN COMIC."

"It's impossible to take your eyes off
the little cross-eyed girl."

She made the white audience laugh,
MUGGING FACES,
GRIMACING, and SIGHING through her exotic jig.
Josephine soaked it up
and kept the job.

After *Shuffle*,
Josephine danced and sang DOWNTOWN
                at the Plantation Club,
but she couldn't sit at a table
                and eat dinner with white folk.
She couldn't enter the front door.

NEGROES used the back door.
　　　Those were the rules.
American rules.
In RESTAURANTS,
　　　NIGHTCLUBS,
　　　　　HOTELS,
　　　　　　TRAINS.
She couldn't try on hats
　　　in the department stores
because that was for
　　　WHITES ONLY.

The VOLCANIC PRESSURE
        kept squeezing tighter,
   way below the surface—
hot magma,
     MOLTEN LAVA,
         TRAPPED WITHIN.

But Josephine made good money
    and sent it home
       for her sisters' schooling,
a piano for little Willie Mae.
ONE DAY there'd be a house for 'em all.

FOR THE FIRST TIME
IN MY LIFE,
I FELT BEAUTIFUL

1925–1936

Performing at the Plantation Club,
GOOFY GLAMOROUS SPARKLING
Josephine caught the eye
of an elegant white lady, Caroline Dudley.
She asked Josephine to perform in
La Revue Nègre in Paris, France.
PARIS? OH, YES.

Get ready for a BLAST. Get ready for JOSEPHINE.

On the ship from New York,
just like any good ole American hotel,
rich white flappers and sleek gentlemen
strolled the **UPPER** decks,
Josephine and the cast of *La Revue Nègre*
strutted the **LOWER** deck—
SEGREGATED.

They all landed in France
        together.
Boarded the French train
        together.
And in the dining car,

*"We were welcomed . . .
we couldn't believe our eyes."*

WERE THE FRENCH COLOR-BLIND?

The ebullient troupe of Harlem Negroes
        poured out of the train
          into rainy Paris,
wearing vermillion, rose, yellow, and green,
plaid pants, polka-dotted skirts and shirts,
outlandish hats tipped over ebony faces,
        and every one of them laughing
          to beat the band.

VIVE LA REVUE!

And from this jovial group
a teenager—bronze, in checkered overalls—
        strode forth,
          smiled, and said,

"So this is Paris!"

JOSEPHINE had arrived
    in the CITY OF LIGHT.

PAUL COLIN,

hired to paint the poster that would advertise

La Revue Nègre,

looked at Josephine,

      A MERE CHORUS GIRL,

with her beautiful ebony body,

like a prizefighter, like a kangaroo,

with rhythm in her hips,

   like a cat ready to strike,

       a volcano about to burst,

with her black painted lips.

He sketched her again and again.

VOILÀ! Josephine became the poster girl.

*"For the first time in my life,
I felt beautiful."*

The poster caused a buzz all over Paris.

                Josephine EFFERVESCED.

Naturally,

      she was chosen to open

      the Charleston number,

            the new Negro American dance.

In rehearsal,

she stalked on stage on hands and feet,

      head down, bottom up,

           the music began.

SHE STOOD.

      She popped her knees, slapped her bottom,

      twirled like a top,

           she skipped,

    SHE SIZZLED.

The chorus of frenzied dancers joined her.

Deep-trapped steam FLASHED and WHISTLED.
Josephine was on fire.
CALL THE FIRE DEPARTMENT.
No! Don't.

Mais oui—
knees squeeze, now fly
arms scissor and splay,

QUELLE SURPRISE!

Word got out.
Opening night
the theater CRACKLED with tension.

A giant dancer lifted Josephine onto the stage.
Like BLACK LAVA, she slid off his back
and faced the audience.
Her deep volcanic core—filled with emotion,
filled with music—ERUPTED.

She shimmied. She shook.
She swiveled and kicked.
Sparks flew.

C'EST MAGNIFIQUE!

"I improvised, crazed with the music.
Even my teeth and eyes burned with fever.
I leapt to touch the sky.
When I regained earth
it was mine alone."

The audience went wild.
A star was born.
NIGHT AFTER NIGHT,
Josephine brought in the crowds—
a dream come true.

People watched and said,
"BLACK IS BEAUTIFUL."

She starred
at the Folies Bergère next.
JOSEPHINE—her name up in lights—
was living a FAIRY TALE.
The theater filled with princes,
painters, diplomats.

The BLACK PEARL
climbed down a palm tree,
wearing a skirt of bananas
and a necklace of shells.
She wriggled like a serpent,
slunk like a panther,
and boxed like a kangaroo.
Mais oui.

Josephine was ALL THE RAGE.
People bought Josephine dolls clad in bananas,
Josephine lipsticks, shoes, perfume, dresses,
Bakerfix hair pomade.
High society tanned to look like Josephine.
All the while,
Josephine bleached her skin with lemons
to look like high society.

She strode down the Champs-Élysées, the heart of Paris,
with her leopard, Chiquita,
each wearing a diamond choker—
       as REGAL as a queen by day
             as WILD as a leopard by night.

She MADE RECORDS,
starred in a movie, then a second and a third,
all Cinderella stories like her own.
RAGS TO RICHES—from lowlife no-life
to Paris high-life.

Josephine danced through Germany, Russia,
Egypt, Sweden, South America.
Her admirers sent her love letters, jewels,
flowers, automobiles.
THEY LOVED HER,
were awed by her abandon,
her daring nature.

She was EXPLOSIVE
and SCANDALOUS.
What fun for Josephine!

In Vienna,
Austrians called her a devil—
a savage—
and riots erupted in the streets.
JOSEPHINE WAS BAFFLED.
Her? A devil?

But she had an idea.

THAT NIGHT at the theater,
dressed in a CREAM-COLORED GOWN
buttoned to the throat,
she sang the Austrians a lullaby,
"PRETTY LITTLE BABY,"
a Negro spiritual—
from a time when Negro slaves
were beaten by
white masters.

WHO COULD CALL *HER* A SAVAGE?

It worked. The Austrians called her an ANGEL.
Another victory for Josephine.
SHE GLOWED.

But she still needed to
CONQUER AMERICA—
so she sailed home,
across the wide Atlantic.

The very first thing,
she divorced Willie Baker—
ended that long-ago marriage.

Then, ON TO THE SHOW.

She starred in the
ZIEGFELD FOLLIES—
the all-white *Follies*—
in New York City.
Josephine bubbled with joy.
She became the FIRST and ONLY
Negro *Follies* star. EVER.
Yet she had to enter her hotel
through the servants' entrance.
All the white stars ignored her.

Worst of all,
critics called her a "Negro wench . . . buck-toothed,"
"a dime a dozen."

She EXPLODED with a SCALDING BLAST.
A *Negro wench* indeed!
But those reviews made her more determined than ever
to fight for her race.

*"Life is a series of summits
and behind each crest looms
another peak to be scaled . . ."*

Back in France she made the most of her volcanic steam.
To recover from the hurt
she became a stunt pilot,
flew loop-the-loops over the countryside,
met a MILLIONAIRE in MIDAIR,
married him.
But he wanted her to live at home—
she divorced him.

"An artist cannot abandon the stage!"

Europe had come to a hard simmer.
In Germany, Jewish people were beaten,
their houses burned.
In 1939, WAR ERUPTED.
Josephine, remembering her childhood
—the FEAR, HATRED, DESPAIR—
made a decision.

*"France has made me what I am . . .
I am prepared to give my life for France."*

JOSEPHINE joined the Red Cross,
ladled soup for the Parisian poor,
flew first aid to Belgium,
        and SPIED FOR FRANCE.

As a star, she traveled everywhere.
In Lisbon, Marseille, Algiers,
at embassy events
        she FLIRTED with friend and foe,
eavesdropped on Nazi enemy officials.

Then, safe in her room,
she wrote it all out in INVISIBLE INK
on her sheet music
or pinned her notes in her underwear
and carried them home to France.

"Who would dare
search Josephine Baker
to the skin?"

A little COUGH in Barcelona turned into
PNEUMONIA in Madrid.
Sent on a mission to Casablanca,
EXHAUSTED and still coughing,
she landed in a North African hospital.
Her visitors—Resistance members—
held secret meetings at her bedside.

Newspapers reported her DEAD.
But she got well.

Well enough to comfort the wounded,
bounce along dirt roads,
get lost in sandstorms,
sleep on the ground like a soldier
with the sand fleas—
all to perform for the U.S. troops.

BLACK soldiers
must sit down FRONT, she said,
together with the white soldiers
in her audience.
Never had she been happier.

Josephine became A HERO.
She helped win the war
for France, the U.S., and their allies.
And she was awarded France's highest honor,
the Légion d'Honneur.
            VIVE LA FRANCE.

JOSÉPHINE

1947–1975

She married JO BOUILLON,
her orchestra leader,
and started to ADOPT CHILDREN
of different races and from
different countries—
from Korea, Japan, Finland, Colombia
came Akio, Janot, Jari, Luis.
Then came Jean-Claude, Moïse, Marianne,
Brahim, Koffi, Mara, Noël,
and finally the youngest, Stellina—

from Canada, Israel, Algeria, Ivory Coast, Venezuela,
and two from France—
   TWELVE CHILDREN IN ALL!

Josephine brought them up in their own religions—
as Buddhist, Shinto, Protestant, Catholic,
Jewish, Muslim, animist.
AT LAST, she felt the whole world was
represented in her family.
   She called them her RAINBOW TRIBE.

They lived in a CHÂTEAU—Les Milandes—
not only a mansion, but a farm and resort,
     where visitors could stay
in a palatial hotel and see for themselves
her rainbow family.

"We'll show the world that racial
hatred is unnatural. . . .
Children of different races can
grow up together as brothers."

But Josephine SPENT MONEY faster than she earned it.
Had her cows' names spelled out in electric
lights in the barnyard:
Jeanette, Rosette, Pervenche, Julie, Honorine.
     QUELLE MERVEILLE! Marvelous!

She bought more LAND,
she bought lavish GIFTS for her children,
she bought designer GOWNS.
        Oh, the bills!

Josephine left her babies behind at Les Milandes
            so she could tour the world,
                so she could DANCE and SING.
She had to support her brood. Her castle. Her tribe.
        Her village.

        Aging and not quite as popular anymore—
some tours weren't such a great success—
        still she loved to perform.
And she loved to arrive home
        with hugs as wide as wings
                and gifts for the children.

She sold her gowns to pay her bills—
        NOT ENOUGH MONEY.
So she sold her art and her jewels.
                        STILL not enough.

Her château was sold from beneath her.
　　　She CLUNG.
They dragged.
　　　She KICKED and BIT.
But she ended up in the street
in the rain,
　　　EVICTED,
her children—homeless,
her health—failing,
　　　her bills—STAGGERING.

Her tribe became a band of vagabonds—
just like her own childhood.
Miserable.
How could this have happened?

They lived off the generosity of friends
and fans like Princess Grace of Monaco.
Josephine was nearly forgotten by her public.
She was OLD.

BUT NOT TOO OLD TO DANCE.

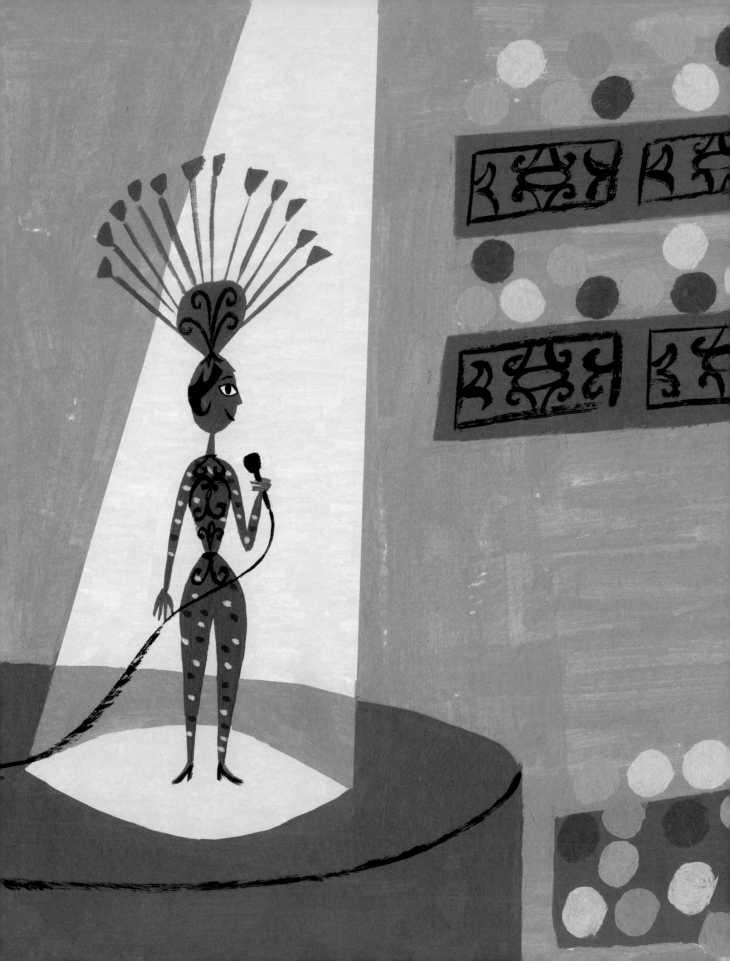

At sixty-seven, she booked a performance
at CARNEGIE HALL in New York City,
the best-known theater anywhere.
How would America receive her this time?

Josephine strode onto the stage
in a sequined bodysuit
and an orange plumed headdress—
four feet high.

The Carnegie crowd
CHEERED till the tears came—
theirs and hers.

She DANCED.
        She SANG.
                She STRUTTED.
Even more cheers and tears at the last bow.

The reviews glowed. AMERICA LOVED JOSEPHINE.
She toured seventeen cities. Everyone loved her.
This was what she wanted—

       success in her first country.

    But the bills kept rolling in for
the Rainbow Tribe.
       The younger children, still in school,
needed their mother.

In Paris she searched for a theater
       to present her NEW SHOW,
JOSÉPHINE.
    Finally, the Bobino theater said yes.
She worked, rehearsed, practiced—
    sang thirty songs
       and DANCED her wild CHARLESTON.

"I wore my heart on my toes
and my soul on my lips.
I sang for the Paris that created me
and I wept as I danced."

She received her best reviews ever.

"THIS IS NOT JUST A COMEBACK.
THIS IS AN ETERNAL RETURN,"
raved *L'Express*.

Paris had opened its arms to Josephine,
once again.
Her doctors said, REST.
She couldn't.

After the opening celebration of *Joséphine*,
she was up half the night,
partying.

VICTORY
was TOO SWEET.
She was ready to go
to the next cabaret.
No one would join her.
Too tired, they said.

The cast took her home to bed.
She went to sleep
and never
woke up.

News spread around the world.
This time it was true.
JOSEPHINE HAD DIED.

Paris gave her the funeral of a QUEEN—

    a hearse covered with flowers

carried her coffin slowly through the streets.

    Hundreds of police

        locked arms

    to stop the crowd

        from crushing the hearse.

A voice in the crowd said,

        "Elle est morte. Elle est immortelle."

SHE IS DEAD. SHE IS IMMORTAL.

As she wished,

    Josephine died breathless, spent,

        at the end of a dance.

    Adieu, Joséphine.

FROM THE AUTHOR

Freda Josephine McDonald was born June 3, 1906, in Saint Louis, Missouri, at the Female Hospital at Manchester Road and Arsenal Street. Josephine's birth was recorded by the head of the hospital, O. H. Elbrecht. Josephine's mother, Carrie, took the baby to her aunt Caroline Crook, who lived in an apartment on Gratiot Street. Once Josephine's siblings were born, the family lived for a time a few houses down in an apartment at 1526 Gratiot Street.

All her life, Josephine believed that people of all races could live together in harmony. After moving to France, she visited the United States to perform and to work tirelessly against racial discrimination, insisting that blacks be integrated with whites in her audiences. She convinced bank presidents, television executives, and store owners to hire black executives and professionals. On August 28, 1963, she spoke alongside Reverend Martin Luther King Jr. on the steps of the Lincoln Memorial, when 250,000 blacks and whites came together for the March on Washington. In order to live what she believed, she adopted the twelve children whom she called her Rainbow Tribe.

With pizzazz and humor, Josephine danced her way out of the slums to eventually become the richest Negro woman in the world, only to lose her fortune and her home due to her characteristic generosity and flamboyance. Josephine Baker died April 12, 1975, but her indomitable spirit—which serves as an inspiration to elevate our own hopes and dreams—lives on.

FROM THE ARTIST

My research for this book consisted of many trips to the Main Library of the San Francisco Public Library. I checked out tons of books on Josephine, the era in which she lived, and the theater posters and costumes of the twenties. My go-to inspiration book was *Josephine Baker and La Revue Nègre*, a collection of lithographs by Paul Colin. This was a reference-only book and couldn't be taken out of the library, so I scanned just about every page and printed them. I also spent many days watching video clips of Ms. Baker dancing and singing. Lastly, I went to Paris! I really wanted to get a sense of Josephine's journey (not that one needs much motivation for Paris!).

But in another way, I've been working on this book my whole life. When I was a child, I remember going on a family trip to New Orleans. It was there, in a gift shop, that I first saw an amazing poster of a woman in a banana skirt. I was mesmerized. My grandmother told me the woman was a wild character and a great dancer named Josephine Baker.

Later I would learn it was an illustration by Paul Colin, and in college, I would come across the film *The Josephine Baker Story*, directed by Brian Gibson, which shared the amazing details of her life. Her courage and endurance moved me. I've thought of her often when facing the obstacles in my own life.

Her life story was a dream come true to illustrate. It is one of fascinating contrasts, steadfast spirit, vibrancy, and wonder. My hope is to have reflected those inspirational aspects in my work and—somehow—to have captured all the richness of her life.

FURTHER READING

Baker, Jean-Claude, and Chris Chase. *Josephine: The Hungry Heart*. New York: Random House, 1992.

Baker, Josephine, and Jo Bouillon. *Josephine*. Paris: Robert Laffont / Opéra Mundi, 1976.

Haney, Lynn. *Naked at the Feast: A Biography of Josephine Baker*. New York: Dodd, Mead, 1981.

Rose, Phyllis. *Jazz Cleopatra: Josephine Baker in Her Time*. New York: Doubleday, 1989.

Schroeder, Alan. *Josephine Baker*. New York: Chelsea House, 1991.

Schroeder, Alan. *Ragtime Tumpie*. Illustrated by Bernie Fuchs. New York: Lillle, Brown, 1987.

QUOTATION SOURCES

Baker, Josephine, and Jo Bouillon. *Josephine*. Translated by Mariana Fitzpatrick. New York: Paragon House, 1988. pp. 16, 24, 28-29, 38, 47, 48, 50, 51-52, 87, 116, 125, 162, 205.

Baker, Josephine, and Marcel Sauvage. *Les Mémoires de Joséphine Baker*. Paris: KRA, 1927. pp. 57, 149.

Baker, Josephine, and Marcel Sauvage. *Les Mémoires de Joséphine Baker*. Paris: Correa, 1949. p. 270.

Haney, Lynn. *Naked at the Feast: A Biography of Josephine Baker*. New York: Dodd, Mead, 1981. pp. 15, 28.

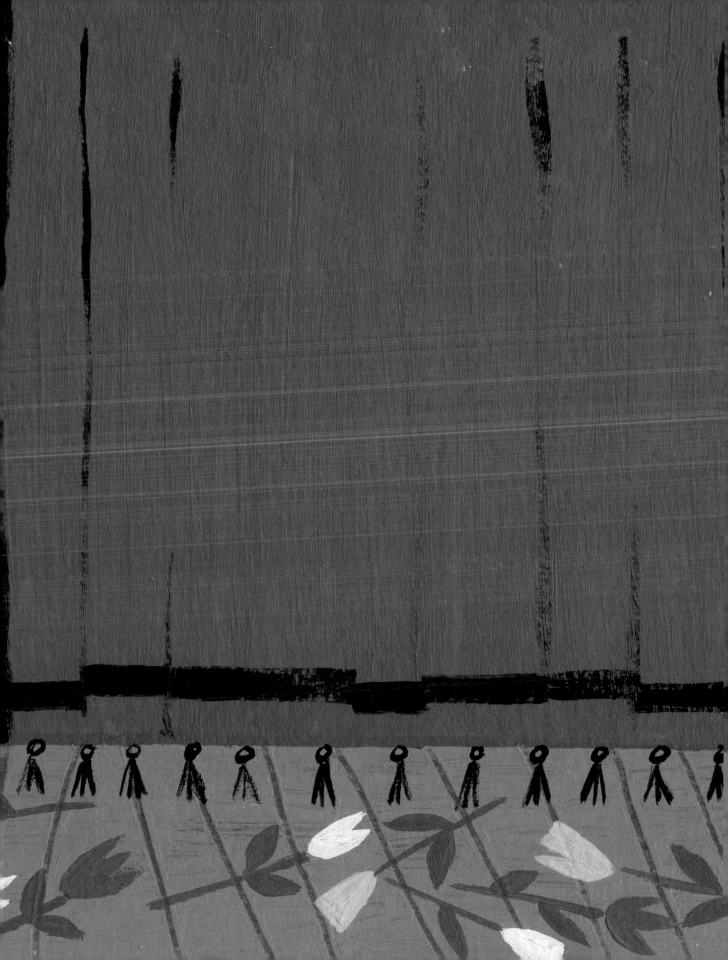